Community Workers

A Chef's Job

Niles Worthington

Cavendish
Square

New York

Published in 2016 by Cavendish Square Publishing, LLC
243 5th Avenue, Suite 136, New York, NY 10016

Copyright © 2016 by Cavendish Square Publishing, LLC

First Edition

Website: cavendishsq.com

This publication represents the opinions and views of the author based on his or her personal experience, knowledge, and research. The information in this book serves as a general guide only. The author and publisher have used their best efforts in preparing this book and disclaim liability rising directly or indirectly from the use and application of this book.

CPSIA Compliance Information: Batch #WS15CSQ

All websites were available and accurate when this book was sent to press.

Library of Congress Cataloging-in-Publication Data

Worthington, Niles.
A chef's job / Niles Worthington.
pages cm. — (Community workers)
Includes bibliographical references and index.
ISBN 978-1-50260-440-8 (hardcover) ISBN 978-1-50260-439-2 (paperback) ISBN 978-1-50260-441-5 (ebook)
1. Cooks—Juvenile literature. 2. Cooking—Vocational guidance—Juvenile literature. I. Title.

TX652.5.W675 2016
641.5023—dc23

2014050270

Editorial Director: David McNamara
Editor: Fletcher Doyle
Copy Editor: Cynthia Roby
Art Director: Jeffrey Talbot
Designer: Alan Sliwinski
Senior Production Manager: Jennifer Ryder-Talbot
Production Editor: Renni Johnson

The photographs in this book are used by permission and through the courtesy of: Ollyy/Shutterstock.com, cover; wavebreakmedia/shutterstock.com, 5; wavebreakmedia/shutterstock.com, 7; Ojo Images/Getty Images, 9; Thomas Northcutt/Getty Images, 11; © istockphoto.com/monkeybusinessimages, 13; Monty Rakusen/Getty Images, 15; wavebreakmedia/shutterstock.com, 17; gerenme/Getty Images, 19; Andersen Ross/Getty Images, 21.

Printed in the United States of America

Contents

Chefs run a restaurant's kitchen.

This is my staff.

4

I plan the menu.

Then I order the **ingredients**.

7

Food must be fresh.

I buy fruit at the market.

9

Food must be **chopped**
before cooking starts.

I am very careful.
The knives are sharp.

11

A head chef teaches cooking secrets.

That's enough sauce.

12

A **pastry** chef bakes desserts.

This cake is for a special day.
It must be perfect.

14

15

I test the food for taste.

This soup is delicious.

Some **recipes** are tricky.

Making this one takes **practice**.

18

This plate is ready to serve.

Enjoy your dinner!

21

New Words

chopped (CHAHPT) To cut food into small pieces with a knife.

ingredients (in-GREE-dee-ents) Food items that go into a recipe.

pastry (PACE-tree) Baked food made with dough that is usually sweet.

practice (PRAK-tiss) To do something over and over to get better at it.

recipe (REH-sih-pee) The steps and ingredients for making food.

22

Index

About the Author

Niles Worthington plays soccer and tennis, and enjoys writing children's books. He also works in his family's pharmacy outside of Chicago, Illinois.

About BOOKWORMS

Bookworms help independent readers gain reading confidence through high-frequency words, simple sentences, and strong picture/text support. Each book explores a concept that helps children relate what they read to the world in which they live.